1. The holiday

The two boys ran down to the beach. They were laughing. The sun was shining, and they were very happy.

Martin, the older boy, pushed his younger brother Sam onto the sand. Then he ran away towards the sea. Sam got up and ran after him. They both ran into the sea and kicked water at each other.

The two boys were brothers. Martin was twelve and Sam was ten. They were on holiday with their mother and father. They were staying in a house about a kilometre from the beach, and every morning they ran down here to swim and play.

It was the best holiday the boys could remember. The beach was very wide and empty, and the sea was clean and full of fish. Both the boys were good swimmers, and every day they swam in the sea for a long time. They wore wetsuits to keep warm, and facemasks so that they could see under water, and sometimes they swam down deep under the water, to watch the fish.

They ran into the sea. The water was cold, but the boys were warm in their wetsuits. They could see hundreds of beautiful fish beneath them - red and blue and green and orange.

There were rocks under the water too. Sam and Martin sometimes swam down and touched them. One of the rocks was very unusual and interesting. It was a large pink rock, about two metres under water, with a large hole in it. Fish swam in and out of the hole, and once Martin swam inside it too, and then came out again. It was very dark inside the hole. Sam swam down too, but he didn't swim inside. Martin laughed at him because he was afraid.

The pink rock was very big, and the other end of it was on the beach. The boys sometimes climbed on it. There was a hole at that end too. You could walk down to it on the sand, and look inside. There was water inside this hole, too.

After swimming, the two boys walked down to the pink rock. They listened to the water inside the hole.

'I'm sure it's the same hole,' Martin said. 'A fish could swim right through this rock. It could start here, and swim out to sea, or it could start in the sea and swim in to us here.'

'But a boy couldn't,' said Sam. 'It's too far. A boy would drown in there.'

Martin laughed. 'You're afraid, little brother!' he said. 'It's not so far. Look, how long is this rock? Eight or ten metres? I can swim twelve metres underwater. I could do it. I wouldn't drown.'

'But it's dark in there,' said Sam. 'And you don't know how big the hole is.'

'That's true,' said Martin. 'But I will do it, one day. I'm not afraid, like you. You'll see.'

Sam said nothing. He didn't want to swim into the hole, but he wanted to be brave. He didn't want Martin to laugh at him.

2. The sea at night

Later that day, the boys went shopping with their father. Their father liked swimming too. He had an unusual camera to use underwater, and today he bought some torches to use in the water, as well. He wanted to photograph the fish at night, he said.

So that evening they all went down to the sea, and swam in the dark sea water. They held torches in their hands, and watched the fish below them. The fish looked grey at night, not red or blue or orange. It was strange, and very beautiful. Sam could see the reflections of the moon and stars on the black sea water, too. 'I am swimming in the sky,' he thought.

3. Into the hole

Next day, the boys came down to the beach again. There was no-one on the beach. Martin was very quiet. He had a bag in his hand. When they were by the sea, he took out two torches and gave one to Sam.

'Here you are, little brother,' he said. 'I'm going to swim through the rock. Are you coming? Or are you afraid?'

Sam did not want to go. But he did not want Martin to laugh at him. So he swam slowly out to the rock, behind his brother. Martin turned in the water, and pointed down, into the water.

'You go first, little brother,' he shouted. 'I'll follow.'

Sam was cold and frightened. He shook his head. 'No,' he said. 'I don't want to. It's too dangerous.'

Martin laughed. 'No it isn't,' he said. 'You're afraid, that's all. You're a coward!'

Sam said nothing. He was afraid, but he was angry and worried too. *'That tunnel is very long and dark,'* he thought. *'We don't know what's in it. And no-one can help us, if we have an accident.'*

Martin pulled his facemask on, and pointed down again, rudely. Sam swam towards him and touched his arm.

'Don't go, please!' he said. 'It's too dangerous. You'll drown!'

But Martin just laughed, pushed him away, and dived under the water. Sam put his facemask on too, and watched his brother swim down towards the hole. Martin swam quickly, kicking hard with his feet. Small bubbles came from his mouth and nose. He swam past some bright green fish, to the bottom of the pink rock. Then he swam into the hole.

4. No answer

Sam watched and waited, but Martin didn't come out. He began to count. 'One ... two ... three ... four ...' He could hear the sound of his heart beating loudly in his ears. '...twenty-three ... twenty-four ...'

Sometimes the two boys swam under the water and held their breath. Each one tried to stay under water longer than the other. Once, Sam had counted ninety-five before he came up. But Martin was older and stronger. He could count a hundred and twenty before he came up.

'... forty-six ... forty-seven ... forty-eight ...' Sam saw something coming out of the hole. It must be - was it Martin's leg? The thing moved very slowly, and went back in again. Then it came out, and swam slowly away. It was a large grey fish.

'... fifty-six ... fifty-seven ...' *'No,'* Sam thought. *'He's not going to come out. He's going to swim right through the rock and come out the other side.'* He began to swim very quickly towards the beach. He was very angry, because he knew Martin would be very pleased with himself. He would laugh at Sam, because Sam hadn't gone first. And he would tell Sam to swim through, to show he wasn't a coward.

Sam swam to the beach and climbed onto the rock. He was running, and he hurt his feet on the sharp rock. He was still counting, too. 'A hundred and one ... a hundred and two ... a hundred and three ...' *'Martin will be out now,'* he thought. *'It's only about nine metres through the tunnel. Martin can swim nine metres easily under water.'* He reached the other hole in the rock, by the beach.

'Hello,' he called. 'What was it like?'

But there was no-one there. A seagull flew away from the rock, screaming loudly. But Sam knew his brother liked to play jokes.

'Come on out, Martin!' Sam called. 'I know you're hiding! Where are you?'

There was no answer. The seagull screamed at him loudly from the sky, and he could hear the sound of the sea on the beach. Nothing else. He walked down onto the sand. He was still counting. 'A hundred and forty-six ... a hundred and forty-seven ...'

'Don't be silly, Martin,' he called. 'Stop hiding and come out now.'

Then he looked at the sand in front of his feet. It was very clean, smooth sand. There were no footmarks on it at all. Martin hadn't walked out of the hole. No-one had. No-one at all.

5. Sam decides

'He must have turned back,' Sam thought. 'He didn't swim through the tunnel so he must have swum back. He must be in the sea again now.'

Quickly, he ran across the rock and looked out to sea. But he could see no boy's head above the water, smiling at him. He couldn't see Martin anywhere.

'Perhaps he's under water again,' Sam thought. But he didn't believe it. 'If he's come out, he'll need air - lots of air,' he thought. 'He won't go under water again. He couldn't. So - he must be still there. Inside the rock.'

Sam felt very cold and frightened. 'Martin is in danger,' he thought. 'He may be drowning - perhaps he's dead already. He needs help, now, quickly!' He looked up the beach, towards the house where his father was. But the house was nearly a kilometre away. It would take twenty minutes to run there and back. That was no good.

'Heeee...elp!' He heard a voice screaming, out to sea. But it wasn't Martin; it was only a seagull, diving for fish.

'Martin needs help now!' Sam thought. 'And I must help him. There's no-one else.'

He dived into the sea and swam out to the end of the rock. When he got there he pulled on his facemask and took a deep breath. He put his face under the water, and then came up again. He was very frightened. The hole in the rock looked like a big black mouth, waiting to swallow him up. He didn't want to go down.

He took another deep breath, and thought of his father and mother, waiting for their two sons to come home. He couldn't go home without Martin. His mother would cry, and his father would say he was a coward. It would be true, too.

He took another deep breath, and then another. *'Just one more,'* he thought. *'Just one more, and then I'll do it.'*

He took one more deep breath, filling his chest with the good, clean sea air. Then he put his face under water, and swam down.

6. No way back!

Down, down towards the hole in the pink rock. The hole grew bigger and darker as he swam towards it. There were plants growing on the side of it, and he saw a crab crawling on the sand. He could hear his heart beating loudly in his ears. The hole opened in front of him, like a big hungry mouth.

'I must be quick,' he thought. *'Very quick. I can only stay under water for ninety seconds. After that I must have air, or I will drown.'* He began counting, ' ... fifteen ... sixteen ... '

He swam inside the hole. Suddenly, it was dark. He switched the torch on, but he couldn't see much. Just rock walls on either side, coming closer. It was frightening. He wanted to scream, but he couldn't open his mouth.

Something touched his face, and for a moment he thought it was alive. He pushed it away with his hand. But it was only a leaf, from a sea plant. ' ... twenty-one ... twenty-two ...'

'I am going too slowly,' he thought. He swam on quickly, into the darkness. The tunnel grew wider, and he could only touch one side with his hand. His chest began to hurt, and he let some air out of his mouth. The air bubble made a loud noise as it floated past his ears. ' ... thirty-nine ... forty ...' He could still see nothing.

'I will go on until forty-five,' he thought. *'Then I'll go back. I have to. If I don't go back then, I'll drown!'*

' ... forty-four ... forty-five.' *'That's it!'* he thought. *'I've tried. I've done my best. But it won't help Martin if I drown too. I'm going to turn back now.'*

He began to turn round. He pushed with his hands against the left of the tunnel, and turned his head to the right. But he couldn't do it. The tunnel was too narrow. He couldn't turn around!

'Heee...elp!' He started to scream and another bubble of air floated out of his mouth into the water. Water came into his mouth and his chest hurt worse than before. There was a terrible pain in his head too.

He pushed hard against the wall of the tunnel, but it was no good. He couldn't turn round!

7. The air pocket

'I'm going to die,' he thought. *'I'm going to drown like Martin.'* But he didn't want to die. Quickly, he swam on, into the darkness. He was still counting. '... seventy-three ... seventy-four ...' Then he hurt his fingers against a rock, and the torch went out. He could see nothing at all. He looked for the switch with his fingers. But he couldn't find it! *'In twenty seconds I'll be dead,'* he thought. *'I'm going to die here alone in the darkness!'* Then he found the switch, and the torch came on again.

He swam very fast, kicking hard with his legs, pulling with his hands against the walls. The sharp rock scratched his fingers, so that blood came, but he didn't notice.

'... eighty-six ... eighty-seven ...' Suddenly, the tunnel went upwards. His head splashed through the surface of the water and hit the roof. But there was air here! His nose was above the water, but his mouth was below it. He shone the torch to the left, and saw a place where the roof was a bit higher. Quickly, he moved there, so that his mouth came out of the water. He filled his chest with great, long, deep breaths of air.

It was an air pocket above the water. It was very small - only his face was above the water. But he could breathe air. He was alive.

8. The end of the tunnel

The tunnel was quite wide here, and Sam could turn round easily. He stayed there for a moment, breathing deeply. The sound of the water was loud in this lonely place. He thought hard.

'I can go back now,' he thought. *'If I take a deep breath and swim back quickly, I will come out of the hole alive.'*

But then something touched his face. He picked it up with his hands and felt it. It was something he knew - a round thing made of rubber. Yes - he knew what it was. A facemask! It must be Martin's facemask! Martin must have left it here.

He thought hard again. *'Martin can't be far away,'* he thought. *'I am sure I have swum six or seven metres already, and the rock is only ten metres long. So he can't be more than three metres away. I can swim three more metres, I'm sure I can. I can swim three more metres forwards, and then, if I don't find him, I can swim back to this place and breathe again. Only ... what if the tunnel is too narrow, and I can't turn around?'*

Sam's heart was beating fast in his chest. He could hear the loud sound of his breathing. But he didn't want to turn back; not now. He took a deep breath, dived under the black water, and swam further into the tunnel.

The tunnel was very narrow. He could touch the walls on each side, and at one place his shoulders touched both walls. But he could feel that it was going upwards. He began counting again.

'... twelve ... thirteen ... fourteen ...' *'I'll go on until thirty,'* he thought. *'That's all. Then I'll turn round - if I can.'*

But he didn't need to count to thirty. At ' ... sixteen ... ' his head came above water again. And this time there was a lot of air. His head came out of the water, and then his shoulders. He shone his torch around. He was in a small cave, about one metre high and two metres across. There were pink rocks everywhere in the cave, and small white crabs and - his brother, Martin!

Martin was sitting on a rock at the side of the cave. He had his hands in front of his eyes, and there was blood on the chest of his wetsuit. But he was alive!

'Martin!' Sam shouted. 'I've found you! Are you all right?'

'No. Stop it - turn that light away.' Martin moved his hand angrily.

'Why? What happened? What's the matter?'

'It hurts my eyes. I hurt my head on something and dropped my torch. I've been sitting here in the dark for a long time. Why didn't you come sooner?'

'I came as quickly as I could,' said Sam, surprised. He shone the torch away from Martin, on the water, and Martin took his hands away from his eyes. Sam could see that he had been crying, and there was blood on his nose. 'I've got your facemask, too - look. You must have dropped it.'

'Thanks,' said Martin. He took the facemask. 'But I don't know how we're going to get out of here. The tunnel is too narrow to go on - look there!'

He pointed to a small hole under the water. It was too small for a boy - only about thirty centimetres across.

'The beach is just through there,' said Martin. 'I'm sure it is - just one or two metres more. But we can't get through. And we can't go back. I'm sure I'd drown if we tried. My chest still hurts from the last time. I can't do it again!'

He put his face in his hands again and began to cry.

Sam looked at him, surprised. He had never seen his big brother cry before. 'It's OK, Martin,' he said.

'We can breathe in the air pocket on the way. Then we just swim straight on. If we got in, we can get out again.'

'Which air pocket?' asked Martin.

'The one about two metres away,' said Sam. 'That's where I found your facemask. Didn't you stop to breathe there?'

'No,' said Martin. 'I just swam straight here. I didn't breathe at all before I got here. It was terrible. The torch went out and I thought I was going to die!'

Sam explained about the air pocket, and Martin looked a little happier. But Sam could see that he was still very frightened.

'Come on,' he said. 'Let's go quickly. We just have to take a deep breath, swim hard, and then we'll be out in the sun again.'

'But I haven't got a torch,' Martin shouted. 'It's all right for you - you've got your torch! But I can't swim through there in the dark!'

Sam thought for a moment. He remembered the terrible time when his torch had gone out. But he had to get Martin out somehow. Quickly, he decided.

'It's all right,' he said. 'You take the torch. You go first - swim to the air pocket, wait for me there, and then you swim out first with the torch. I'll follow you. I'll be able to see the light in front of me.' He smiled and gave the torch to Martin.

Martin looked at his little brother, very surprised. Then he shook his hand. 'Thanks, Sam,' he said. 'You're - you're a really great brother, you know. Really brave. I'll never forget this.'

Then he put on his facemask, took a deep breath, and dived down into the black water.

'Wait for me at the air pocket!' called Sam. But it was too late. Martin had gone, and so had nearly all the light. Sam could just see a tiny light, like a small star, far away underwater. And even that small star was going away fast.

9. Into the darkness

Sam put on his facemask and dived down into the black water. He dived in so quickly that he forgot to take a deep breath. But he had to go, quickly. *'If that light goes,'* he thought, *'I won't be able to see anything. I won't even be able to find the air pocket.'*

It was very hard to swim in the dark, and soon his chest began to hurt, because he hadn't taken a deep breath. He swam fast, down, down into the darkness. But then the light was there in front of him, shining through the water. He saw his brother's legs in front of him. Sam swam quickly up towards the roof of the tunnel. Yes! Martin had found the air pocket, and he was waiting there for him.

The two brothers breathed deeply in the tiny air pocket. Their heads were very close together, and the air was very bad, but it was air. Martin smiled at Sam.

'Are you OK, little brother?' he said.

'I'm OK,' Sam said. He tried to smile back, but his face hurt too much.

'All right, then. Let's go!' said Martin. He took a deep breath, and dived away into the darkness, taking the torch with him.

'Wait!' shouted Sam. His voice sounded loud in the tiny air pocket. It was already black, and the light was going. *'But I can't swim yet,'* he thought. *'I haven't got enough air in my chest. I must breathe more first.'*

So he waited, alone in the darkness, and breathed deeply four times. It was completely dark now. All the light from the torch had gone, and Sam could see nothing at all. He held his hand in front of his eyes, but he couldn't see it. He had never been so alone in his life before.

But he didn't think about it. He took one last deep breath, and dived down into the black water.

It was not easy. He could not see the walls, and so he had to touch things with his hands. He began to count again, and swam as quickly as he could. '... thirteen ... fourteen ... fifteen ...'

'If I am going the wrong way, I will drown in here,' he thought. *'I'll never find the air pocket again without the torch.'*

But then the water in front of him began to get lighter. He could see a tiny star of light at the end of the tunnel. He swam quickly towards it, and it grew larger. '... twenty-nine ... thirty ...'

He could see the walls of the tunnel now, and a fish swimming past the end of it. He kicked harder with his feet, swam faster, and suddenly he was outside the hole, and back in the sea again! He swam up, up, up, towards the sunlight. Little blue and red fish swam past him, and bubbles came out of his mouth and nose.

And then his face was out of the water, in the clean, fresh air again! The sun was shining on him, seagulls were flying in the sky, and his brother Martin was floating in the water near him.

Sam took long, deep breaths of the lovely, fresh, clean air. He floated on his back, and swam slowly towards the beach. Martin swam beside him. They walked out of the water, lay down on the warm sand, and laughed.

Far away at the end of the beach, they could see their father walking towards them. Martin looked at Sam, and gave him back his torch.

'Thanks, little brother,' he said. 'You're the bravest little brother in the world. You saved my life.'

Words in this Book

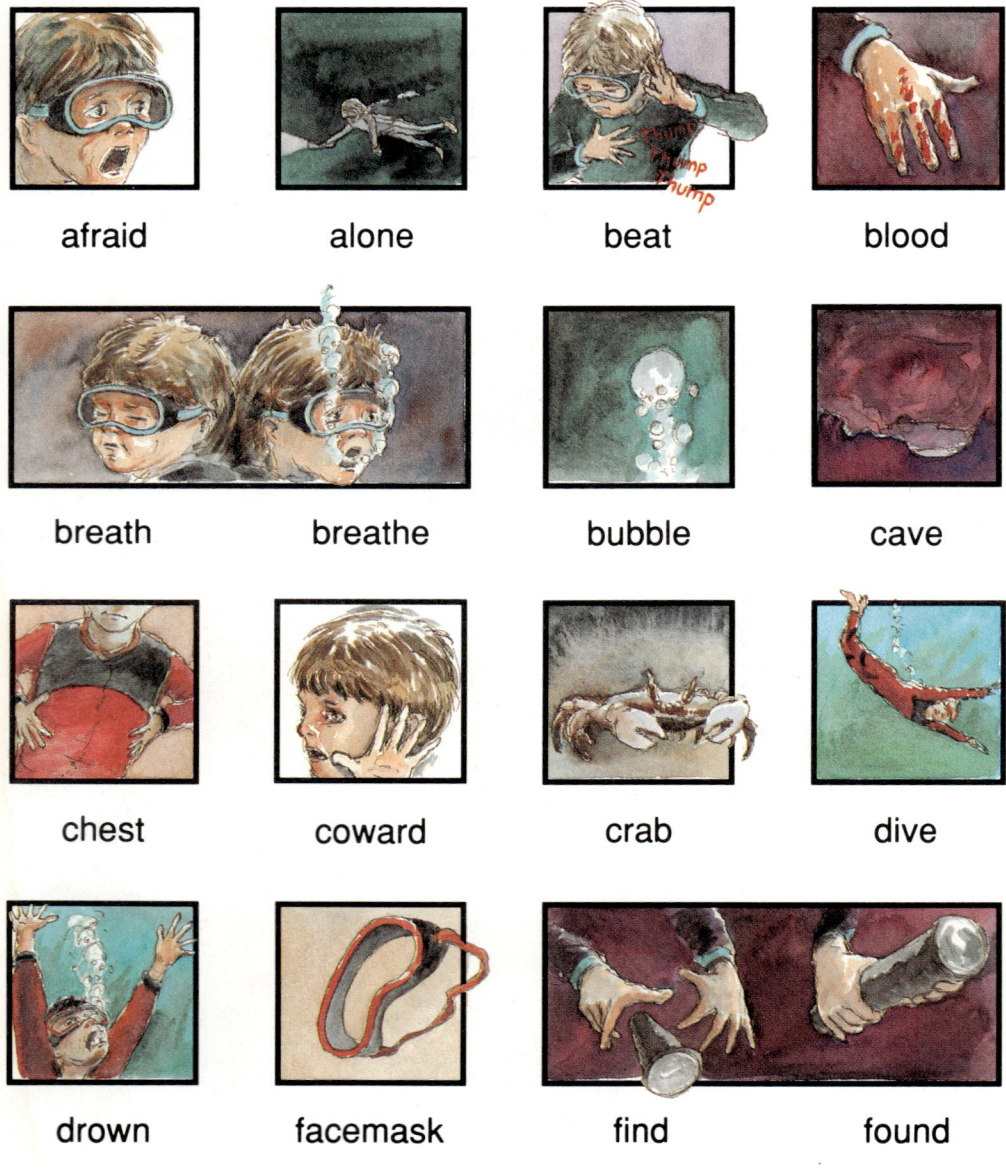

afraid

alone

beat

blood

breath

breathe

bubble

cave

chest

coward

crab

dive

drown

facemask

find

found

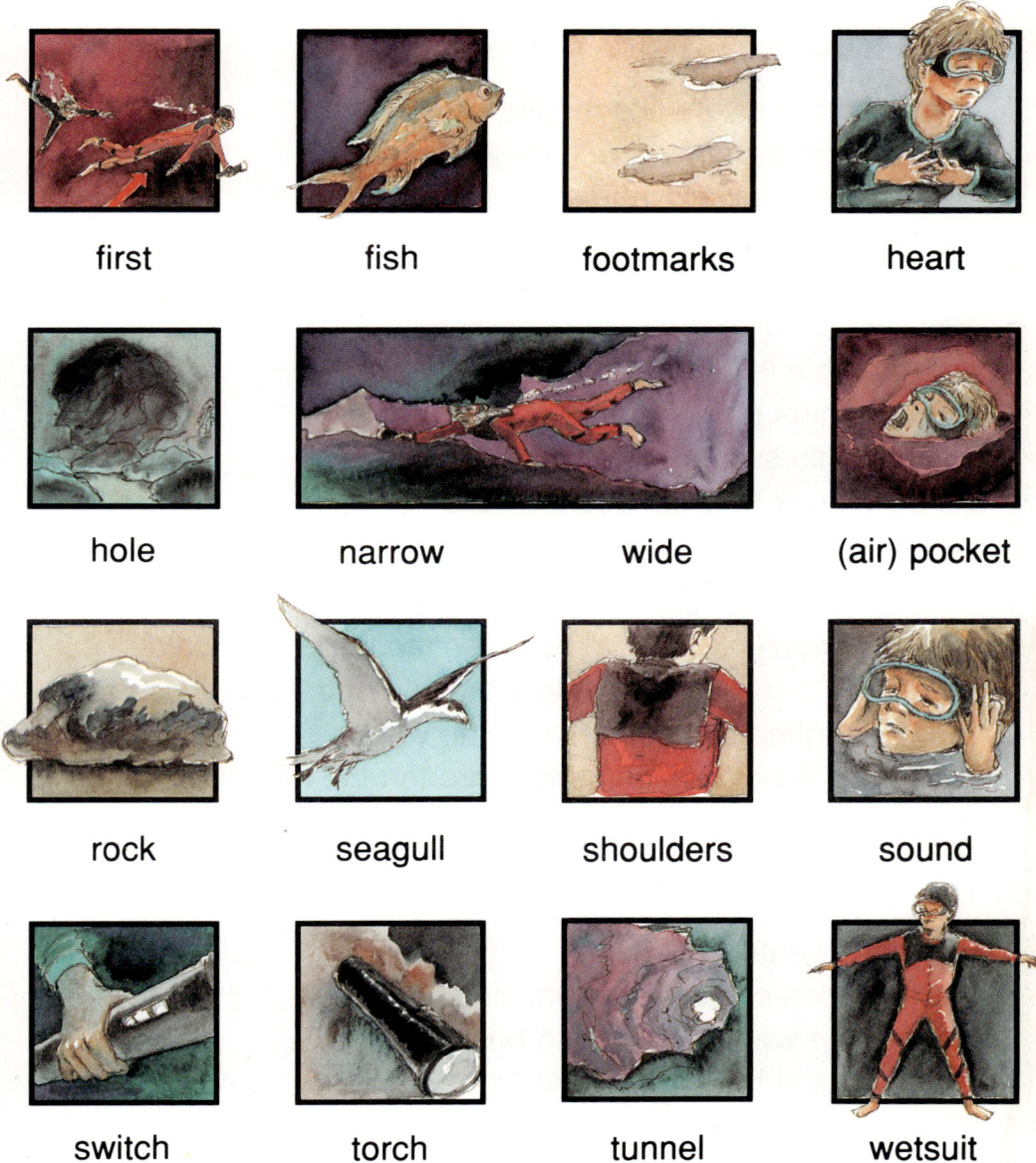

first

fish

footmarks

heart

hole

narrow

wide

(air) pocket

rock

seagull

shoulders

sound

switch

torch

tunnel

wetsuit

Questions

1. The holiday

A. Give short answers like the first two.
1 Were the boys happy? *Yes, they were.*
2 Did they walk towards the sea? *No, they didn't.*
3 Were they good swimmers?
4 Was the water warm?
5 Was it light inside the hole in the rock?
6 Was the hole in the rock above the water?
7 Did the tunnel go right through the rock?
8 Could Martin swim 50 metres underwater?
9 Did Sam want to swim into the hole?

B. Add the missing words.
1 The house was about a . . . . from the beach.
2 The boys wore . . . . because the water was cold.
3 They wore . . . . to help them see underwater.
4 Martin laughed at Sam because he was . . . .
5 Sam said: 'A boy couldn't swim through the tunnel. He
  would . . . . in there.'

2. The sea at night

Finish these sentences.
1 Their father's camera was unusual because . . . .
2 Their father went shopping to buy some . . . .
3 The boys and their father used the torches to . . . .
4 When Sam looked at the black sea he could see . . . .

3. Into the hole

Answer these questions.
1 Why did Sam swim so slowly out to the rock?
2 What did Martin ask Sam to do ?
3 What was the rude word that Martin used about his brother?
4 What did Sam say to try to stop his brother?
5 What came out of Martin's mouth as he dived?

4. No answer

A. Choose the best answer.
1 Sometimes the boys swam under water and:
   (a) held their hands.
   (b) held their breath.
   (c) shut their eyes.

2 What did Sam see coming out of the hole in the rock?
   (a) seaweed
   (b) Martin's leg
   (c) a fish

3 When Sam realised Martin wasn't coming out, he felt:
   (a) very angry.
   (b) very pleased.
   (c) afraid.

4 Sam knew Martin hadn't come out at the other end because:
   (a) the hole was full of sand.
   (b) there was sand in front of his feet.
   (c) there were no footmarks on the sand.

B. Complete these sentences.

1 Sam could hear the sound of . . . .

2 Martin could stay underwater longer than Sam because . . . . .

3 Sam thought Martin would laugh at him because . . . .

4 When no-one answered, Sam thought his brother was . . . . . .

5 When Sam saw the clean smooth sand he realised . . . .

5. Sam decides

Which of these sentences are true and which are untrue?

1 Sam couldn't see Martin in the sea.

2 Sam ran to get help from his father.

3 Sam heard a seagull screaming.

4 Sam took one deep breath and dived to the bottom.

6. No way back!

Complete these sentences.

1 As Sam swam towards the hole, it grew . . . .

2 The hole looked like a . . . .

3 'I can only stay underwater for 90 seconds,' Sam thought.
'So I must . . . .'

4 When a leaf from a sea plant touched his face, Sam thought
it . . . .

5 He couldn't turn round because . . . .

7. The air pocket

Answer these questions.

1 Why did the torch go out?

2 How did Sam swim fast in the narrow cave?

3 Why did he move to the left?

8. The end of the tunnel

A. Add the missing words.

1 When Sam was in the air pocket, he breathed . . . .

2 The facemask was round and made of . . . .

3 Sam thought, 'I may not be able to turn round, because the tunnel is too . . . .'

4 Martin's chest had . . . . on it.

5 Martin and Sam were sitting in a small . . . .

6 Martin didn't think Sam was a coward now. He said he was really . . . .

B. Answer these questions.

1 'Martin can't be far away,' Sam thought. Why did he think this?

2 When was Sam going to turn back?

3 How big was the cave?

4 Sam gave Martin two things. What were they?

5 Why couldn't they swim through the rock to the beach?

6 What could Sam see, when Martin swam away underwater?

9.   Into the darkness

Which of these sentences are true and which untrue?

1 Sam took a deep breath before he dived.

2 He swam very fast into the darkness.

3 Martin was waiting for Sam because Martin couldn't find the air pocket.

4 There was good air in the air pocket.

5 Sam tried to smile at Martin.

6 Little blue and red bubbles floated past Sam.

7 Sam swam beside Martin towards the beach.

Oxford University Press
Walton Street, Oxford OX2 6DP

Oxford New York Toronto Melbourne Auckland
Petaling Jaya Singapore Hong Kong Tokyo
Delhi Bombay Calcutta Madras Karachi
Nairobi Dar es Salaam Cape Town

and associated companies in
Berlin Ibadan

OXFORD and OXFORD ENGLISH are trade marks
of Oxford University Press

ISBN 0 19 422419 8

© Oxford University Press 1990

First published 1990
Second impression 1990

Illustrated by Cliff Wright

Typeset by Pentacor Ltd, High Wycombe, Bucks

Printed in Hong Kong